To Michelle
From Gary & Joyce
Christmas 1978

The Night Before Christmas

CLEMENT C. MOORE

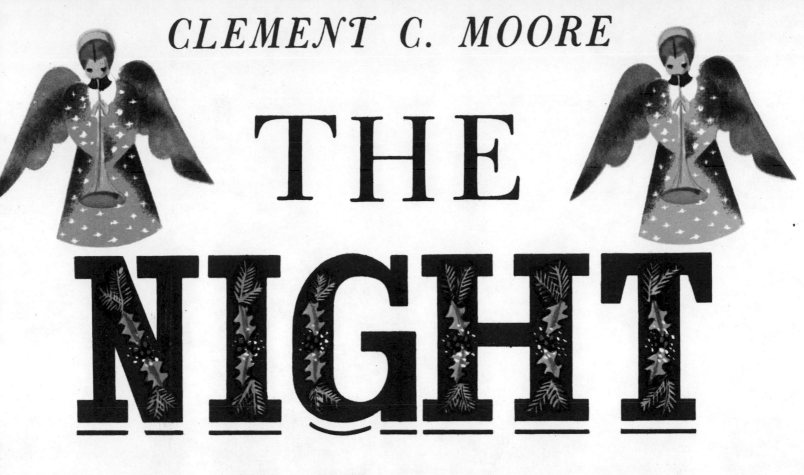

THE NIGHT BEFORE

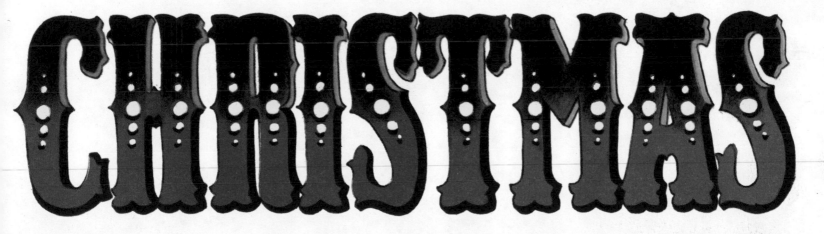

CHRISTMAS

ILLUSTRATED BY LEONARD WEISGARD

GROSSET & DUNLAP • PUBLISHERS • NEW YORK

COPYRIGHT 1949 BY GROSSET & DUNLAP
ISBN: 0-448-04205-3   1978 PRINTING
LITHOGRAPHED IN THE U.S.A.

'Twas the night before Christmas, when all through the house

Not a creature was stirring, not even a mouse;

The stockings were hung by the chimney with care, In hopes that St. Nicholas soon would be there;

The children

all snug

While visions

danced

were nestled
in their beds,
of sugarplums
through their
heads;

And Mamma in
  her 'kerchief,
  and I in my cap,
Had just settled
  our brains
  for a long winter's nap,
When out on the lawn
  there arose such

  a clatter,
I sprang from my bed
  to see what was
  the matter.
Away to the window
  I flew like a flash,
Tore open the shutters
  and threw up
  the sash.

The moon on
   the breast of
   the new-fallen snow
Gave a lustre of
   midday to
   objects below,
When, what to my
   wondering eyes
   did appear,
But a miniature
   sleigh, and
   eight tiny reindeer,

With a little old driver
      so lively and quick,
I knew in a moment
      he must be St. Nick.
More rapid than eagles
      his coursers they came,
And he whistled, and shouted,
      and called them by name:
"Now, Dasher! now, Dancer!
      now, Prancer and Vixen!
On, Comet! on, Cupid!
      on, Donder and Blitzen!
To the top of the porch!
      to the top of the wall!
Now dash away! dash away!
      dash away, all!"

As leaves that before
the wild hurricane fly,
When they meet with an obstacle,
mount to the sky,

So up to the housetop
    the coursers they flew,
With the sleigh full of toys,
    and St. Nicholas too—

And then in a twinkling,
 I heard on the roof
The prancing and pawing
 of each little hoof.

As I drew in my head,
 and was turning around,
Down the chimney St. Nicholas

 came with a bound.

He was dressed all in fur,
from his head to his foot,
And his clothes were all tarnished
with ashes and soot;
A bundle of toys he had
flung on his back,
And he looked
like a peddler
just opening
his pack.

His eyes—how

his dimples

His cheeks

his nose

hey twinkled!

now merry!

were like roses,

like a cherry!

His droll little mouth

was drawn up like a bow,

And the beard

on his chin

was as white as

the snow;

The stump of a pipe
he held tight in his teeth,
And the smoke it encircled
his head like a wreath;
He had a broad face
and a round little belly
That shook when he laughed,
like a bowl full of jelly.

He was chubby and plump,
a right jolly old elf,
And I laughed when I saw him
in spite of myself;
A wink of his eye and
a twist of his head
Soon gave me to know
I had nothing to dread;

He spoke not a word, but
went straight to his work,
And filled all the stockings;
then turned with a jerk,
And laying his finger
aside of his nose,
And giving a
nod, up the
chimney
he rose.

He sprang to his sleigh,

to his team gave a whistle,

And away they all flew

like the down of a thistle.

But I heard him exclaim

ere he drove out of sight—

"Happy Christmas to al

and to all a Good Night!"